LIKE THE NEW MOON I WILL LIVE MY LIFE

Like the New Moon
I Will Live My Life

Robert Bly

INTRODUCTION BY THOMAS R. SMITH

EDITED BY DENNIS MALONEY

WHITE PINE PRESS / BUFFALO, NEW YORK

White Pine Press
P.O. Box 236
Buffalo, New York 14201
www.whitepine.org

Acknowledgments appear on page 218, which constitutes an extension of this copyright page.

Publication of this book was made possible, in part, by grants from Amazon.com ; the National Endowment for the Arts, which believes that a great nation deserves great art; and with public funds from the New York State Council on the Arts, a State Agency.

Cover art: *New Moon* by Simon Xianwen Zeng. Used by permission of the artist.

First Edition

ISBN: 978-1-935210-64-1

Printed and bound in the United States of America.

Library of Congress Control Number: 2014947460

TABLE OF CONTENTS

from *This Tree Will be Here for a Thousand Years* (1979)

Uncollected Poems

ROBERT BLY'S LESS-TRAVELED ROAD

Thomas R. Smith

Like many American poets of his generation, Robert Bly came of age admiring older formal poets such as Yeats and Frost, who deeply color his earliest published efforts. Yet as a young poet, also in keeping with his generational experience, Bly soon recognized the necessity and opportunity for breaking new ground. Where to look for that? The Imagists were old news. European surrealism, one of the more durable 20th century movements, was already a few decades old. A 1956 Fullbright allowed Bly to travel to Norway to translate Norwegian poetry, and in the Oslo public library he discovered Pablo Neruda, among other major poets outside the Anglo-American tradition. Back in the States, Neruda's protean example energized Bly's efforts to bring more of the "wild" image's power into American poetry via translations and poems of "the new imagination" in his magazine *The Fifties*, founded in 1958.

At some point, though, attention to Bly's native Midwestern landscape called for an approach differing from Neruda's. Bly remembered in his *Paris Review* interview: "When I wrote poems in those years, I was not someone like Neruda, trying to feel my way back through centuries of human suffering and human grief. I'm sitting beneath a tree and realizing that I'm happy doing that. . . ."

Bly has vividly described a fresh sense of openness in the poetry scene of the 1950s, perhaps attributable to America's optimism at having won WWII and returned to peacetime, "the simple delight people felt in air, wind and poems when there was no war. . . ." Young poets also gained in possibility what they lost in structure as the old formal style lost its hold at midcentury. That charmed period proved short-lived; the 1960s brought a return to wartime and with it a bitter social and political turbulence tearing apart all conventional assumptions of American post-war progress and stability. While the Nerudian-Spanish surrealism was well-suited for exposing underground psychic fault-lines of Vietnam-era America, what of the poet's spiritual health? How was that to be maintained?

Besides the South American, Spanish and Scandinavian poets, Bly had also been reading Robert Payne's great anthology of Chinese poetry, *The White Pony* (1947), as well as translations of the ancient Chinese poets by Arthur Waley, Kenneth Rexroth, and others. The critic Howard Nelson has written insightfully of the influence of the Chinese poets on Bly's first collection, *Silence in the Snowy Fields,* published in 1962, to which he ascribes a "radical plainnness" worthy of those poets. Bly's comment in a 1968 interview supports Nelson's view of the importance of the Chinese influence to Bly's maiden effort: "The ancient Chinese poetry still seems to me the greatest poetry ever written."

Bly has said that poems of depth and silence can function as political commentary because "the political poem comes out of the deepest privacy." Australian scholar Dennis Haskell agrees that in their reflectiveness the *Snowy Fields* poems "gain something of a moral stance, since they provide the poet with a basis for judging the nation's psychic life." The informality and spontaneity of the Chinese-influenced style also relieved what James Wright identified as "the anxiety of the poet's egotism" permeating the academic poetry of the 1950s. Wright, like Bly, discovered freedom in the spaciousness both men first admired in spare Chinese poems and then adapted to their own work: ". . . it's not only that there seems to be some kind of space around the words, but that space somehow makes its possible for me to enter the poem, and live there if I feel that I want to do so."

It is this Chinese-influenced strain of Bly's work with its room for movement, spontaneity and openness that *Like the New Moon I Will Live My Life* most amply showcases in its nearly 190 poems, almost two-thirds of which arguably fit this category. These poems all pre-date 1980, after which we notice a clear shift which I'll discuss shortly. Generally dating from early to mid-point in Bly's career, they are in many cases available only in out-of-print chapbooks commanding high prices on the collector's market. A few have never appeared outside of their original magazine publications. Since Bly has chosen to de-emphasize this body of work in his most recent selected poems, *Stealing Sugar from the Castle*, giving far more weight to later developments, such as his adaptation of the Middle Eastern ghazal, we might view the present collection as a kind of back road running parallel to the more-traveled route of Bly's selected poems.

The first poems one encounters in this book are reprinted from *The Lion's Tail and Eyes: Poems Written Out of Laziness and Silence* (1962), a collaborative volume undertaken along with compatriots James Wright and William Duffy the same year Wesleyan University Press brought out *Silence in the Snowy Fields*. Bly's stylistic range of that era is fully displayed here: "Traveller Leaves Appomatox" exemplifies the historical surrealism of *The Light Around the Body*; "Sparks of the Body" wouldn't be out of place in Bly's Jungian autobiographical long poem "Sleepers Joining Hands"; and finally poems such as "Reading the Translations of William Hung" and "The Grass-Headed Lion" represent the relaxed yet alert vein of his work inspired by the ancient Chinese poets.

In Bly's Chinese-style poems, an essentially meditative consciousness affirms the importance of work, solitude, and acceptance of grief and suffering to spiritual well-being. These poems collectively suggest a practice for maintaining spiritual wholeness in psychically dismembering times when wide-spread "death-mother" energy claims many victims. Eschewing mainstream temptations, Bly does not swerve from his commitment to transcendent vision.

These poems, however, are not really about any of the concerns mentioned above. They are not even what we would call "nature" poems. Rather, they are poems of the moment, in which phenomena are observed, both outside and inside the poet, in a state of heightened attentiveness. Neither are they poems of the larger gesture, although Bly has written many of those as well. The classical Chinese poem does not recognize the Western distinction between poet and subject, and so the real subject of the poem becomes the mysterious unity of opposites. Bly's poems in *Like the New Moon I Will Live My Life* fully participate in that inseparability of inner and outer, subject and object. In "After a Day of Work" we feel a harmony of the poet and his world:

> How lightly the legs walk over the snow-whitened fields!
> I wander far off, like a daddy-longlegs blown over the water.
> All day I worked alone, hour after hour.
> It is January, easy walking, the big snows still to come

Disciplined work is the necessary pre-condition for the vision these poems achieve, often in a very few lines. It's difficult to tell whether Bly's "work" is in fact the work of writing or of attention itself. In "Walking and Sitting," he reports: "That's odd — I am trying to sit still, / Trying to hold the mind to one thing." Given Bly's frequent dedication to an actual meditation practice, the ambiguity may be intentional.

Effort can as likely give way to a sense of futility as of satisfaction. Bly concludes "Writing Again" on a discouraged note: "Well that is how I have spent this day. / And what good will it do me in the grave?"

Because they register the mercurial ephemera of experience, we may notice many reversals, contradictions and contrasts in poems written within close proximity in time of one another. Compare the last-quoted lines above to these, written at the end of another day, from "Sleeping Faces":

Letters sink into the desk,
The desk sinks away, leaving an intelligence
Slowly learning to talk of its own suffering. . . .
My life is a blessing, a triumph, a car racing through the
    rain.

Also belonging to this period are Bly's "doing nothing" poems, whimsically expressive more of a Taoist spontaneity than a Buddhist discipline. In fact, as the poet Allan Cooper has pointed out to me, Bly's "A Doing Nothing Poem" directly quotes Shiki's haiku, translated by R. H. Blyth whom Bly in the 1970s also thoroughly absorbed:

Doing nothing at all,
The sea-slug has lived
For eighteen thousand years.

Solitude in which to work is at a premium at this point in Bly's life, involving complicated negotiations for time away from family and demands of the frequent reading tours that become a staple of his livelihood in the 1960s and 1970s. One imagines the matter somewhat more mixed than Bly admits in "Living a Week Alone," though the relief of escape from other duties is evident: "My family is still away. No one is home. / How sweet it is to come back to an empty house —" At times we suspect Bly of overstating his case: "Every day I did not spend in solitude was wasted." ("After Long Busyness") And yet Bly's need for introverted solitude, often referred to in these poems as "privacy," is real enough: "When your privacy is beginning over, / How beautiful the things are that you did not notice before!" ("Like the New Moon I Will Live My Life")

In his solitude, Bly is also susceptible to prompts of imagination. Thus in these pages his "privacy" gives us many small gems of imaginative perception, accessible only to those who have undertaken the labor of preparing the conscious mind to receive the gifts of the unconscious. A delightfully high-spirited example is "A Cricket in the Wainscoting":

That song of his is like a boat with black sails.
Or a widow under a redwood tree, warning
Passersby that the tree is about to fall.
Or a bell made of black tin in a Mexican village.
Or the hair in the ear of a hundred-year-old man!

The discipline of poetry does not necessarily entail ecstatic or exuberant states. We recall that Bly's master's thesis at the University of Iowa was a poetry collection titled *Steps Toward Poverty and Death*. A recognition of the grief and suffering in life has stood from the beginning as a foundation for Bly's labor, both poetically and spiritually. Acceptance of suffering is also, of course, a tenet of Buddhist thought, which saturates the poems of Bly's Chinese and Japanese models such as Tu Fu and Issa. In "Thinking of 'The Autumn Fields,'" after Tu Fu's poem, Bly says, perhaps a little too idealistically: "In the second half of life a man accepts poverty and illness; / Praise and blame belong to the glory of the first half."

In "Amazed by an Accumulation of Snow," Bly reiterates his triple discipline of work, solitude and acceptance: "I had been singing alone in my darkened house / About a man who agrees to endure suffering." "Alone" is a word we notice frequently in Bly's "Chinese" or *Snowy Fields* poems. In "The Visit of Two Birds," written in this period but only published in 2005, Bly first experiences joy while observing a hawk "floating past with the sun through his wings," perhaps on his farm in western Minnesota. Later though, after driving a half-hour to a lake in search of greater privacy, Bly concludes:

> After I'd been alone four hours,
> A heron, with the cry of those
> Who awkwardly suffer, and are ignored,
> Settled near me on the shore.

Bly has written in his recent poem, "Growing Wings": "A pain that we have earned gives more nourishment / Than the joy we won at the lottery last night." It may be in Bly's Lutheran cultural DNA to distrust the easy pleasure and value the hard-won sorrow. In that respect, "The Visit of Two Birds" can be seen as a kind of ars poetica.

That Bly chose to highlight this Chinese-inflected aspect of his work in his debut volume speaks to its personal importance to the poet. He continued to write a few poems in the *Snowy Fields* style each year, an accumulation which eventually became *This Tree Will Be Here for a Thousand Years* (1979). A projected third volume of "Snowy Fields" poems never fully materialized, though the briefer *The Urge to Travel Long Distances* (2005) can be seen as an attenuated cousin. Undoubtedly there are still others waiting to be collected.

In the 1980s we notice in Bly's work a turning away from the Midwestern-pastoral mood of *Snowy Fields*. This is the period when he began to publish his love poems, represented here by work originally included in the chapbooks *Out of the Rolling Ocean* and *In the Month of May*. Around this time, the word "you" begins to appear more often in Bly's poems. The love poem requires an abandonment of, if not solitude, then solitariness, for the sake of the beloved; thus we hear in the voice of these poems a new note of intimacy. In this more expansive mode, Bly finds a different way to draw on his Chinese models, employing the tactful imagery of Chinese poetry to suggest physical love:

> Once I loved you only a few minutes a day.
> Now it is smoke rising, the mushroom left by the birch,

The horse's forefoot, the way the minnow stirs silver
As he turns carrying his world with him.

> ("The Minnow Turning")

In his chapbook *Holes the Crickets Have Eaten in Blankets*, mourning the death of his adoptive son Sam Ray, Bly openly grieves in some of his most emotionally naked lines:

Sam, now where have you gone?
I held you often on my knees,
My arms circling you, and we
Were friends, helping each other.

> ("After Your Death")

These poems, not preserved in any of Bly's major collections, perhaps for fear of sitting uncomfortably with other themes, now find a worthy home in *Like the New Moon I Will Live My Life*.

Finally, at least glancing attention must be given to a change visible in Bly's poetry in the 1980s, registered in the later selections of this book, a renewal of interest in sound and form. If Bly's stance prior to 1980 was a vehement refusal to acknowledge formal considerations, by the late 1970s and early 1980s he seemed to take as a serious challenge his old friend Donald Hall's 1974 assertion that "If Bly could write his poems in amino acids or bird calls, he would just as lief; the spirit matters to him, and not the shoulders of consonants."

To this playful accusation, Bly responded with an original poetic form expressly designed to explore the possibilities of sound, which he calls a *ramage* (from a French musical form, derived from the Latin for branch, or ramify). This eight-line form focuses especially on the tiny vowel-consonant partnerships Bly has dubbed "sound particles." One will find a handful of these small "concertos" or "improvisations," as Bly has sometimes identified them, toward the end of this book.

Sound is a key element of poetic form, and the 1980s saw a near-complete revolution in Bly's approach to form in his first major collection of that decade, *The Man in the Black Coat Turns*, introducing into his work intricate stanzas reminiscent of Marianne Moore's. It's intriguing to think that the "black coat" of the title may be a veiled concession to Hall's charge that Bly has been something of a puritan in his neglect of poetry's sound-pleasures.

In "A Dream of William Carlos Williams," a complicated exchange takes place between Bly and the elder poet. When Bly remarks that Williams "fell out" of form, Williams is startled to hear it. Could this be a subconscious recognition that Bly has misunderstood WCW's refusal of traditional poetic form? The poem ends: "You asked about form in my poems. I found myself / Lying, saying I cared nothing about form. . . ." The dream cunningly allows Bly to re-examine his old position. In the double ramage "The Gaiety of Form" Bly makes clear his new position:

> The chosen vowel reappears like the evening star
> There, in the solemn return the astronomers love.
> When "ahm" returns three times, then it becomes
> A note; then the whole stanza turns to music.

Thus Bly's turn away from earlier solitude toward relationship and community in his later work is appropriately mirrored by his return in the 1980s to a more conscious use of sound and form.

As I've noted in this introduction, the present gathering disproportionately highlights one strand among many in Bly's prolific opus; yet there is enough breadth, especially in the selections that begin and end this volume, to suggest the richness and variety of the whole. I hope these remarks will serve to clarify for the reader the greater arc of Bly's work within which these poems fall.

Robert Bly's "undeclared sureness of self," as Dennis Haskell aptly put it, has guided him with an extraordinary degree of confidence through the continual dynamic change that has made his writing career such a bracing adventure for those who have followed it over the long term. In a 1972 interview in *The Lamp in the*

Spine, Bly said, "A Chinese poem or a great work of art, (which gets through the skin) all it does is touch a real thing . . ." In learning from the ancient Chinese poets how to clear away the mind's dulling distractions, attend to essential realities of the world, and cultivate a sensitivity to those other worlds both inside and beyond us, Bly has consistently touched the pulse of the real all along its bandwidth, from the visible to the invisible, and brought a multitude of real things into his poems to strengthen and enrich his readers' sense of the grandeur of living.

NOTES

"When I wrote poems in those years...."
Interview with Francis Quinn, *The Paris Review*, 154, Spring 2000, page 56

"the simple delight people felt"
ibid., page 51

The critic Howard Nelson
Howard Nelson, *Robert Bly: An Introduction to the Poetry*, Columbia University Press, New York, 1984, page 5

"The ancient Chinese poetry still seems...."
Robert Bly, "Two Halves of Life" in *Talking All Morning*, University of Michigan Press, Ann Arbor, 1980, p. 129

"the political poem comes out of the deepest privacy"
Robert Bly, "Leaping Up into Political Poetry" in *Forty Poems Touching on Recent American History*, Beacon Press, Boston, p. 11

Australian scholar Dennis Haskell
Dennis Haskell, "The Modern American Poetry of Deep Image," *Southern Review*, Vol. XII, No. 2, July 1979, University of Adelaide, Australia, page 155

"the anxiety of the poet's egotism"
James Wright, "Chinese Poetry and the American Imagination," *Ironwood* 17, Tucson, AZ, 1981, p. 20

"it's not only that there seems to be some kind of space...."
Wright, ibid., p. 20

Shiki's haiku
R. H. Blyth, *Haiku, Volume 4, Autumn-Winter*, The Hokuseido Press

and Heian International, Tokyo and San Francisco, 1952, 1982, p. 1,265

"Growing Wings"
Robert Bly, *My Sentence Was a Thousand Years of Joy*, HarperCollins, New York, 2005, page 23

Donald Hall's 1974 assertion
Donald Hall, "Notes on Robert Bly and Sleepers Joining Hands," in *Goatfoot Milktongue Twinbird: Interviews, Essays, and Notes on Poetry, 1970-76*, University of Michigan Press, Ann Arbor, 1978, page 137

"undeclared sureness of self"
Haskell, op. cit., page 152

"A Chinese poem or great work of art"
Robert Bly, quoted in Haskell, page 140

from
The Lion's Tail and Eyes

Silence

The fall has come, clear as the eyes of chickens.
Strange muffled sounds come from the sea,
Sounds of muffled oarlocks,
And swampings in lonely bays,
Surf crashing on unchristened shores,
And the wash of tiny snail shells in the wandering gravel.

My body also wanders among these doorposts and cars,
Cradling a pen, or walking down a stair
Holding a cup in my hand,
And not breaking into the pastures that lie in the sunlight.
This is the sloth of the man inside the body,
The sloth of the body lost among the wandering
        stones of kindness.

Something homeless is looking on the long roads—
A dog lost since midnight, a small duck
Among the odorous reeds,
Or a tiny box-elder bug searching for the windowpane.
Even the young sunlight is lost on the window pane,
Moving at night like a diver among the bare branches
        silently lying on the floor.

Reading the Translations of William Hung

I am doing nothing, so I read old poems.
It is early spring. Strangely twisted leaves emerge
        from their buds.
Tu Fu's spirit enters into the bones of old men
        leaving for battle.
Walking around, I feel joy as I see old boards
        scattered on the new grass.

The Grass-Headed Lion

The smoky morning has come.
The night is over.
The grass-headed lion has gone back to his den.

The ship has sailed over the horizon,
The red wheat pours out,
The rowers are lifting their hats in the morning heat.

The river flows past roots and old wharfs.
Silk waits in attics.
The small snails come out to greet the sun.

Traveller Leaves Appomatox

Nothing can be done, until the pirates hoist their
        black flags,
And the mole, sleeping, rises crowned with leaves,
The wild milk foams on shipboard,
And the masts group in a vast and sleeping harbor.
Boars are tearing at the roots of trees
In Tennessee,
Where the long shrouds of the leaves cover the
        bones of men,
And muskets cry out in the steaming woods all
        night,
And hollow trees, and rotted stumps, and buckles
        cry out!

Dirty papers cover the streets of Harlem;
I see the half-painted signs,
The anguish,
The conviction that tomorrow will be like today,
That birds must be in cages,
The certainty that the fish is thirsty—
In New York the cables lie all
Breathing at the sides of streets,
Night at the sides of streets,
Ready to be placed in concrete;
Leaving Appomatox, Traveller is moving
Through the stumpy fields, among mosquitoes in the
        shape of men;
We are in pain;
It is the old pain—
I hear Hoover crying in his sleep,
And sooty trees kneel in Spanish churches, lighting
        the candles with their branches.

Dark earth, thirty-five feet deep,
Flows beneath the trees,
Dark flowers floating on the underground lakes,
Ground water is slowly drifting through the honey-
      combs of shale;
This water is our water,
It is a new water, pure through many poisoned
      stones.

Sparks of the Body

Yes, I am the son, new born in the Lutheran wastes of Minnesota, like an eye! Writhing on the ground, newly woken from sleep, like a slave who hates the sparks in the body! Woken at winter dark to row in the frozen ocean air, or to scrub the closets in a castle made of black sticks—

Is the body prowling on the shore of the grave?—like a heap of stones resentful it is not a wing. Where are the friends who are not with us? Heavy smoke of sleep rolls from the body. How long before it begins to burn? And She? Is She in the same anguish?

Evolution From the Fish

This grandchild of fishes
Holds in him a hundred thousand tiny stones,
This nephew of snails, naked
On a bed with a smiling woman, blazing
Under marble roofs, moves toward his own life
Like fur walking. He is fur, mammoth fur growing
As the leaves fall, or slim Indian hands living
Their play of disturbed snakes, heartless life
Passing each other, fur that climbs a wall,
Kissing a woman's skin, leaning against a pillar,
He moves toward the animal, the animal with furry head!

What a joy to smell the flesh of a new child!
Like new grass, and the long man with the student girl,
Coffee, pale waists, the spirit moving around them,
Moves, dragging a great tail, into the darkness.
And ourselves, blazing up, drawing spiny fish
As we sleep, we throw off the white stones!
The sea serpent ascends with spiral motions,
The man closes a door, sluggish thought enters the diamond
To sleep. O do not stop me now! Let me raise
My hands, fire passes through the soles of my feet—
I am curving back into the mammoth pool!

from
Jumping Out of Bed

Turtle Climbing from a Rock

For Wang Hui-Ming

How shiny the turtle is, coming out
Of the water, climbing the rock, as if
Buddha's body were to shine!
As if swift turtle wings swept out of darkness,
Crossed some barriers,
And found new eyes.
An old man falters with his stick,
Later, walkers find holes in black earth.
The snail climbs up the wet trunk glistening
Like an angel-flight trailing long black banners.
No one finds the huge turtle eggs
Lying inland on the floor of the old sea.

Like The New Moon I Will Live My Life

When your privacy is beginning over,
How beautiful the things are that you did not notice before!
A few sweetclover plants
Along the road to Bellingham,
Culvert ends poking out of driveways,
Wooden corncribs, slowly falling,
What no one loves, no one rushes towards or shouts about,
What lives like the new moon,
And the wind
Blowing against the rumps of grazing cows.

Telephone wires stretched across water,
A drowning sailor standing at the foot of his mother's bed,
Grandfathers and grandsons sitting together.

Some November Privacy Poems

I am comforted
By a crack in dry ground
Nearly smoothed over with winter dust.

How marvellous to look out and see
The boulders
That have been gloomy since the earth began
Now with a faint dusting of snow.

Mist: no one on the other shore.
It may be the trees I see have consciousness
And this desire to weep comes from them.

Most birds have gone south.
Grass heels over in wind.
The feminine hooves of the horse
Stand side by side as he eats.

On A Moonlit Road in the North Woods

I sit on the forest road,
Cross-legged.
I am an oyster
Breathing on his own shore.

Cars seldom use this road.
I looked up and down,
            no car coming, none would,
Perhaps for hours...

All day my thoughts ran on in small rivulets
Near some bigger flood,
Several times water
            carried me away;
Then I was a cedar twig,
            a fish scale...

And what does the oyster think
On this forest road?
He thinks of his earlier life,
Of meeting her again.

The Walnut Tree Orchard

(An answering poem in which Wang Wei writes the first
poem, then his friend P'ei Ti writes a poem answering it.)

Wang Wei: In the old days the serious man was not an
    "important person."
He thought making decisions was too complicated
    for him.
He took whatever small job came along.
Essentially he did nothing, like these walnut
    trees.

P'ei Ti: I soon found doing nothing was a great joy to me.
Look, you see, here I am! Keeping my ancient
    promise.
Let's spend today just strolling around these
    walnut trees.
The two of us will nourish the ecstasies Chuang
    Tzu loved.

The Hill of Hua-Tzu

Wang Wei: The birds fly away into the air that never ends;
                The magnificence of fall comes back to the
                    mountain.
                Whenever I walk up or down Hua-Tzu hill,
                My whole body feels confusion and inner
                    suffering.

P'ei Ti: The sun goes down; there is wind sound in the
                    pines.
                Walking home I notice dew on the grass.
                The white clouds look up at me from the tracks
                    of my shoes.
                The blue from the mountain touches my clothes.

Chrysanthemums

(planted for Tao Yuan Ming, who likes them)

1.
Tonight I rode again in the moonlight!
I saddled late at night.
The horse picked his way down a dead-furrow,
Guided by the deep shadows.

2.
A mile from the yard the horse rears,
Glad. How magnificent to be doing nothing,
Moving aimlessly through a nighttime field,
And the body alive, like a plant!

3.
Coming back up the pale driveway,
How calm the wash looked on the line!
And when I entered my study, beside the door,
White chrysanthemums in the moonlight!

After Long Busyness

I start out for a walk at last after weeks at the desk.
Moon gone, plowing underfoot, no stars; not a trace of light!
Suppose a horse were galloping toward me in the open field?
Every day I did not spend in solitude was wasted.

Six Images for Death

Death throws a shadow on our shadow, as if it were a tree.
We then are pasture grass the cows eat unevenly.
We are a weight on a string swaying from the motion of the
     planet.
We are a rock tunnel through which chill air rushes.
Mammoths feel the air rise through their hollow legs.
The leaves above the grass pick up the wind and rustle.

A Night in December

On this windy December night two children lost their way.
"Birds ate the womb-shaped seeds we dropped in the moonlight."
("You know we left so early the moon was still out.")
"Come in, do not be frightened, children."

How odd that I feel a connection between the feminine
And this windy December night! Or is it the feminine?
When Paris took Helen away, he kept the moon in a pouch.
Inside the salmon's stomach, the cook finds the wedding ring.

"Come in, do not be frightened, children!"
Why do men need this fear? Some are torn in pieces,
Other men lengthen out years on islands...
This night calls: men will die for this night.

Sleeping Faces

Tonight the first fall rain washes away my sly distance.
I have decided to blame no one for my life.
This water falls like a great privacy.
Letters sink into the desk,
The desk sinks away, leaving an intelligence
Slowly learning to talk of its own suffering.
The muttering of thunder is a gift
That reverberates in the roof of the mouth.
Another gift is a child's face in a dark room
I see as I check the house during the storm.
My life is a blessing, a triumph, a car racing through the rain.

The Creek by the Luan House

Wang Wei: Autumn rain and sudden winds.
                        The water plunges, bouncing off the rocks.
                        Waves leap aimlessly over each other.
                        The white heron is alarmed and lands.

P'ei Ti: A man could hear the water-sound far off.
                        I walk down looking for the ford.
                        Ducks and egrets swim away, and then
                        Veer back, longing to be near people.

The Magnolia Grove

For Michael Bullock

Wang Wei: The mountain receives the last sunshine of fall.
                Flocks fly off following the first that leaves.
                Occasionally something emerald flashes in the
                        trees.
                The evening dark has nowhere to settle down.

P'ei Ti: Settling down at dusk from the dome of light
                Bird voices get mingled with the river sounds.
                The path beside the river winds off into the
                        distance.
                Joy of solitude, will you ever come to an end?

Another Doing Nothing Poem

There is a bird that flies through the water.
It is like a whale ten miles high!
Before it went into the ocean,
It was just a bit of dust from under my bed!

Walking in Ditch Grass

The spring wind blows, dissatisfactions
And mad architects, two-mile long tails—

And my shoes, like whales
Eat the grass, they sweep through
The grass, eating
Up the darkness.

The night is windy. Sleek cows fly
Across the sky. Samson
Is angry. It must be this grass we need
To balance out dissatisfactions,
This grass, blowing, open, and uneven.

Tongues Whirling

You open your mouth, I put my tongue in,
And this wild universe-thing begins!

Our tongues together are two seagulls
         whirling high above the Great Lakes,
Two jellyfish floating under a Norwegian moon!

Suddenly we are with the fallen leaves,
         blowing along the soaked roads.
My hand closes so firmly around you
And I feel the sea rising
         and falling
As we go ashore...

We are two turtles with wings!

We are rolling together, head down,
Through oceans of mother air!

We are two tumbleweeds hurrying through the universe.

A Doing Nothing Poem

After walking about all afternoon
Barefoot, in my shack,
I have grown long and transparent...
Like the sea slug
Who has lived alone doing nothing
For eighteen thousand years.

The Poem

Coming nearer and nearer the resonating chamber
The poem begins to throw itself around
Fiercely,
Silent stretches of snow,
Grass waving for hundreds of miles.

Intent pierces into hard wood, which grows dense
From inside, something mad penetrates
The wood,
Something alive, something
Human, like a violin that reverberates with thought.

A fierce intent that nature does not know of
Drives inside the poem,
Changes it,
Thickens it with sober weight;
It is something dense, a human madness.

Looking at Cloud Banks Below the Plane Window

Hills of cloud, mountains of mist below.
What are they? Troll-heads,
Tufts of forgetfulness,
Childhood stories, dreams of someone's death.

Perhaps a burbling up of blind affection...
The clouds are affectionate creatures
With their backs turned to us,
Crouched over a smiling landscape beneath.

How different these tuffy bodies are from ours!
They are secretive, but do not cling,
Are not afraid of a storm,
Willing to dissipate in the wind...

Two Drinking Songs

versions of Tao Yuan Ming

I.

I built my hut where people live
And yet I hear no traffic noise or sound of wheels.
Could you tell me what is happening?
An aloneness gathers around the soul that is alone.
I pick chrysanthemums underneath the east hedge,
The mountains to the south are clear.
The mountain air at sunset is so wonderful,
And the birds coming home, one after the other.
In all these details there are secret truths;
But when I try to shift to language, it all slips away.

2.

Such a strong color on the late chrysanthemums!
The stalk sways stoutly, flower wet with dew, open.
Wandering drunk in this beauty, who cares about my sorrows.
I have left excitement behind, and what is not done.
Alone, I take a drink.
The bottle tilts by itself when the cup is empty.
When the sun goes down, all bustle stops,
And the birds on their return call from the leaves.
I walk around my study shouting and proud
Because I can take up this life again.

from

Old Man Rubbing His Eyes

October Frost

Last night the first heavy frost.
Now the brave alfalfa has sobered.
It has folded, as if from great heat,
And turned away from the north.
The horse's winter coat has come
Through the bark of the trees.
Our ears hear tinier sounds,
Reaching far away east in the early darkness.

Writing Again

Oval
Faces crowding to the window!
I turn away,
Disturbed—

When I write of moral things,
The clouds boil
Blackly!
By day's end
A room of restless people,
Lifting and putting down small things.

Well that is how I have spent this day.
And what good will it do me in the grave?

Fall Poem

There are eyes in the dry wisps of grass,
And invisible claws in the rooster's eyes,
The patient feet of old men in the boards left out all summer.

Something is about to happen!
Christ will return!
But each fall it goes by without happening.

The end of the pickup disappears down the road,
The pigweed bent over like abandoned machines...

Sitting In Fall Grass

All day wind had called me,
Oceans, a yellow line streaking
Across the sky,
Bones thrown out of graves.

I walked to my sitting place,
I sat down.

When I close my eyes, what
Piles of bones I see!
Ruined castles,
Trampled cinnamon,
Crinoline crushed in long grass.

And voices that say,
I am not like you...
I must live so...condemned
By an old yellow lion...

Night Farmyard

The horse lay on his knees sleeping.
A rat hopped across the scattered hay
And disappeared under the henhouse.
There the chickens sat in a stiff darkness.

Asleep they are like bark fallen from an old cottonwood.
Yet we know their soul is gone, risen
Far into the upper air about the moon.

Dawn in Threshing Time

The three-bottom plow is standing in a corner of a stubble field. The flax straw lies exhausted on the ground.

The dawning sun slants over the wet pigeon grass, so that the slope of highway ditches is like a face awakening from sleep.

The oat stubble is shiny. The farmer puts on his jacket and goes out. Swaths still to be combined are wet. Every morning as he gets up after thirty he puts on besides his jacket the knowledge that he is not strong enough to die, which he first felt deep in his wooden cradle at threshing time.

Reading in Fall Rain

The fields are black once more,
The old restlessness is going.
I reach out with open arms
To pull in the black fields.

All morning rain has fallen
Steadily on the roof.
I feel like a butterfly
Joyful in its powerful cocoon.

I break off reading:
One of my bodies is gone!
It's outdoors, walking
Swiftly away in the rain!

I get up and look out.
Sure enough, I see
The rooster lifting his legs
High in the wet grass.

Insect Heads

These insects, golden
And Arabic, sailing in the husks of galleons,
Their octagonal heads also
Hold sand paintings of the next life.

To Live

"Living" means eating up particles of death,
        as a child picks up crumbs from around the table.
"Floating" means letting the crumbs fall behind you on the path.
To live is to rush ahead eating up your own death,
        like an endgate, open, hurrying into night.

Cornpicker Poem

I.

Sheds left out in the darkness,
Abandoned granaries, cats merging into the night.

There are hubcaps cooling in a dark yard.

The stiff-haired son has slouched in
And gone to bed.
A low wind sweeps over the moony land.

2.

Overshoes stiffen in the entry.
The calendar grows rigid on the wall.

He dreams, and his body grows limber.
His is fighting a many armed woman,
He is a struggler, he will not yield.
He fights her in the crotch of a willow tree.

He wakes up with jaws set,
And a victory.

3.

It is dawn. Cornpicking today.
He leans over, hurtling
His old Pontiac down the road.

Somewhere the sullen chilled machine
Is waiting, its empty gas cans around it.

Prophets

There are fields of white roses
With prophets asleep in them—
I see their long black feet.

A Cricket in the Wainscoting

That song of his is like a boat with black sails.
Or a widow under a redwood tree, warning
Passersby that the tree is about to fall.
Or a bell made of black tin in a Mexican village.
Or the hair in the ear of a hundred-year-old man!

Digging Worms

Here I am, digging worms behind the chickenhouse,
The clods fall open when I hit
Them with a tine, worms fall out…

Dreams press us on all sides, we stagger
Along a wire, our children balance us
On their shoulders, we balance their graves
On ours.

Their graves are light. And we unwind
From some kind of cocoon made by lovers…
The old tires we used to swing on,
Going faster, around and around, until

With one lurch we grow still and look down at our shoes.
Last night I dreamt my carelessness started stones dis-
Lodging near a castle. The stones
Did not hurt my shoulders when they hit and went through,
But the wall of the castle fell.

Walking and Sitting

That's odd—I am trying to sit still,
Trying to hold the mind to one thing.
Outdoors angleworms stretched out thin in the gravel,
While it is thundering.

A Long Walk Before the Snow Began

1.

Nearly winter. All day the sky gray. Earth heavy.
The cornfields dead. I walk over the soaked
Cornleaves knocked flat in rows,
A few grains of white sleet on the leaves.

2.

White sleet also in the black plowing.
I turn and go west—tracks, pushed deep!
I am walking along with an immense deer.
He passed three days ago.

3.

I reach the creek at last, nearly dusk.
New snow on the river ice, under willow branches,
Open places like the plains of North China,
Where the mice have been, just a half hour ago.

4.

It must be that I will die one day!
I see my body laid out.
A woman whose face is hidden stands near my body.
A column of smoke rises from Vonderharr's field.

A Dream On The Night Of The First Snow

I woke from a first-day-of-snow dream.
I met a girl in an attic,
      who talked of operas, intensely.
Snow has bent the poplar over nearly to the ground,
New snowfall widens the plowing.
Outside, maple leaves float on rainwater,
      yellow, matted, luminous.
I saw a salamander...and took him up...
He was cold. When I put him down again,
      he strode over a log
With such confidence, like a chessmaster,
      the front leg first, then the hind
      leg, he rose up like a tractor climbing
      over a hump in the field
And disappeared toward winter, a caravan going deeper into
      mountains,
Dogs pulling travois,
Feathers fluttering on the lances of the arrogant men.

A Walk

It is a pale tree,
All alone in January snow.
Beneath, a cottonwood shoot
Eaten pale by a rabbit...

Looking up I see the farmyards with their groves,
The pines somber,
Made for winter, they knew it would come...

And the cows inside the barn, caring nothing for all this,
Their noses in the incense hay,
Half drunk, dusk comes as it was promised
To them by their saviour.

from
The Loon

The Loon

From far out in the center of the naked lake
The loon's cry rose...
It was the cry of someone who owned very little.

Wind

The grasshopper on the cliff
Leaps about
Recklessly, two hundred feet above the water!

Alone

The river moves silent under the great trees.
A fish breaks water,
And then, a few feet farther down, again.

The Car

So much love, those who love us,
Those whom we love,
The afternoon shadow thrown by a car.

August Sun

Strips of August sun come in through shutters.
Baskets of unanswered letters
Lie on chairs.
Some foolish man must live here!

Near Dark

The fishermen
Slam their car doors, and drive
Away from the lake.

Near Morris

The old river willow
Is angry at her saplings
For allowing sheep to eat them.

Kabekona Lake

Lots of men could sleep
On those fir branches
Swaying near the widow's house!

Winter Grass

Grass standing. Falling, snow pauses
Above it...and then settles.
The late spring snow swirling down.

Fall

The spider disappears over the side
Of the yellow book, like
A door into a room never used.

Grass

The cottonwood leaves
Lie naked on the grass
Still chilled from the night.

Storm Windows

How beautiful the pale sky of the west is
In the storm windows
Not yet put up
As I go by!

Ducks

Two white ducks waddle past my door
Moving fast:
They are needed somewhere!

from
This Tree Will Be Here
for a Thousand Years

Women We Never See Again

There are women we love whom we never see again.
They are chestnuts shining in the rain.
Moths hatched in winter disappear behind books.
Sometimes when you put your hand into a hollow tree
You touch the dark places between the stars.
Human war has parted messengers from another planet,
Who cross back to each other at night,
Going through slippery valleys, farmyards where the rain
      has washed out all tracks,
And when we walk there, with no guide, saddened, in the dark
We see above us glowing the fortress made of ecstatic blue stone.

November Fog

This private misty day
With the lake so utterly cast down, like
A child.
The long anxious wheels
Churning in sand,
The pale willow leaves shedding light
Around the "pale bride and groom."

Ant Heaps by the Path

I love to stare at old wooden doors after working,
The cough the ant family makes in ground,
The blackish stain around screwheads.

How much labor is needed to live our four lives!
Something turns its shoulders. When we do work
Holes appear in the mountainside, no labor at all.

Amazed by an Accumulation of Snow

I had been singing alone in my darkened house
About a man who agrees to endure suffering.
The door opened, I was amazed to see the air thick;
The horse had turned his rump to the north.
Snow flows along the valleys of his back.
The white roof stood calmly among the black trees.

It is a shock that snow fell over the whole farm
While the singer remained private and alone in his house.
It is as if the African heron craved of buffalo horn
Suddenly would open his mouth and call,
Or a bell from under glass would lift and ring.
The horse's hoof kicks up a seashell, and the farmer
Finds an Indian stone with a hole all the way through.

Pulling a Rowboat Up Among Lake Reeds

In the Ashby reeds it is already night,
Though it is still day out on the lake.
Darkness has soaked into the shaded sand.
And how many other darknesses it reminds me of!
The darkness the moment after a child is born,
Blood pouring from the animal's neck,
The slender metal climbing toward the moon.

Moving Books to a New Study

First snow yesterday, and now more falling.
Each blade has its own snow balanced on it.
One mousetrack in the snow ahead,
The tailmark wavering in
Between the footprints. Dusk in half an hour.

Looking up I see my parents' grove.
Somehow neither the Norwegian culture
Nor the American could keep them warm.
I walk around the barn the long way
Carrying the heavy green book I love through the snow.

Driving My Parents Home at Christmas

As I drive my parents home through the snow,
Their frailty hesitates on the edge of a mountainside.
I call over the cliff,
Only snow answers.
They talk quietly
Of hauling water, of eating an orange,
Of a grandchild's photograph left behind last night.
When they open the door of their house, they disappear.
And the oak when it falls in the forest who hears it
        through miles and miles of silence?
They sit so close to each other…as if pressed together
        by the snow.

After a Day of Work

How lightly the legs walk over the snow-whitened fields!
I wander far off, like a daddy-longlegs blown over the water.
All day I worked alone, hour after hour.
It is January, easy walking, the big snows still to come.

Walking Where the Plows Have Been Turning

> "The most beautiful music of all is the music of what happens."
> —old Irish tale

for Gioia Timpanelli

Some intensity of the body came to me at five in the morning. I woke up, I saw the east pale with its excited brood. I slipped from bed, and out the back door, onto the sleek and resigned cottonwood leaves. The horses are out, eating in the ditch...I walk down the road toward the west.

I notice a pebble on the road, then a corn-ear lying in the ditch-grass, then an earthbridge into the cornfield. I walk on it to the backland where the plows turn, the tractor tires have married it, they love it more than the rest, cozy with bare dirt, the downturned face of the plow that looked at it each round...

In the risen sun the earth provides a cornhusk in one place, a cottonwood tree in another, for no apparent reason. A branch has dropped onto the fence wire, there are eternities near, the body free of its exasperations, ready to see what will happen. There is a humming in my body, it is jealous of no one. The cricket lays its wings one over the other, a faint whispery sound rises up to its head...which it hears...and disregards...listening for the next sound...

July Morning

The day is awake. The bark calls to the rain still in the cloud.
"Never forget the lonely taste of the white dew."
And woolen robed drummers call on the naked to dance,
All the particles of the body shout together.

Sitting on the disc, the morning dove coos a porch,
       then a cathedral,
Then the two arms of the cross!

He gives the nose, then the head, then the two ears
      of this rabbit
Hopping along the garden,
Then his death...

After that we will be alone in deep blue reaches of the river.

An Empty Place

Empty places are white and light-footed. "Taking the road" means being willing to die, as the pigeon grass clump, that dies so quietly. There is a joy in emptiness. One day I saw an empty corncob on the ground, so beautiful, and where each kernel had been, there was a place to live.

The eyes are drawn to the dusty ground in fall—
Small pieces of crushed oyster shell,
Like doors into the earth made of mother-of-pearl;
Slivers of glass,
A white chicken's feather that still seems excited by the warm
        blood,
And a corncob, all kernels gone, room after room in its endless
        palace...
This is the place of many mansions,
Which Christ has gone to prepare for us.

Prayer Service in an English Church

Looking at the open page of the psalm book,
I see a ghostly knot floating in the paper!

Circles within circles on the page, floating,
Showing that a branch once lived there!

Looking at the knot long and long,
I hear the priest call on the Saviour to come again.

The old around me keep on singing...
If the Saviour is a branch, how can he come again?

And the last day...
The whispers we will make from the darkening pillow...

Fishing on a Lake at Night

Someone has left a light on at the boathouse
To guide the fishermen back after dark.
The light makes no sound as it comes.
It flies over the waves like a bird with one wing.
Its path is a boatful of the dead, trying to return to life
Over the broken waters.

                    And the light
Simply comes, bearing no gifts,
As if the camels had arrived without the Wise Men.
It is steady, holding us to our old mountain home,
Now as we watch the moon rises over the popple forest.
It too arrives without fuss,
It goes between the boards around the pulp-cutter's house—
The same fence we pass through by opening the gate.

Night of First Snow

Night of first snow.
I stand, my back against a board fence.
The fir trees are black at the trunk, white out on the edges.
The earth balances all around my feet.

The apple trunk joins the white ground with what is above.
Fir branches balance the snow.
I too am a dark shape vertical to the earth.
All over the sky, the gray color that pleases the snow mother.

A woman wades out toward the wicker basket, floating,
Rocking in darkening reeds.
The child and the light are half asleep.
What is human lies in the way the basket is rocking.

Black and white end in the gray color of the sky.
What is human lies in the three hairs, caught,
The rabbit left behind
As he scooted under the granary joist.

Solitude of the Two Day Snowstorm

Supper time...I open the door and go out...something blowing among the tree trunks...our own frail impulses go to shelter behind thin trees, or sail with the wind—

It is night...this is the time when after long hours alone, I sit with my family, and feel them near...at what I want to do I fail fifty times a day, and am confused...at last I go to bed.

At five I wake, strong wind around the north bedroom windows, I get up and go out, there is dust of snow on yesterday's ice. The snow grows gradually, the winds do not stop.

By afternoon, I lie listening to the wind...still going on...rising and wailing, sometimes with a sudden sweep, a woman's skirt pulled swiftly along the floor...at other times it gives a steady growl without anger, like the word "Enoch"...I stand up and look out.

The crow's head I found by the bridge this summer, and brought home, sits on the window sash, the one black thing before all that white. The head looks intense, swift, decided, the beak partly open, the eyes sunk. Among that soft white, the head looks like a warship...snow-blankets suddenly fall off the window screen behind him...

Frost Still in the Ground

I walk out in the fields; the frost is still in the ground.
It's like someone just beginning to write, and nothing has
       been said!

The shadows that come from another life
Gather in folds around his head.

So I am, all at once. What I have
To say I have not said.

The snow water glances up at the new moon. It is
Its own pond. In its lake the serpent is asleep.

Late Moon

The third week moon reaches its light over my father's farm,
Half of it dark now, in the west that eats it away.
The earth has rocks in it that hum at early dawn.
As I turn to go in, I see my shadow reach for the latch.

A Dream of Retarded Children

That afternoon I had been fishing alone,
Strong wind, some water slopping in the back of the boat.
I was far from home.
Later I woke several times hearing geese.
I dreamt I saw retarded children playing,
   and one came near.
And her teacher, the face open, hair light.
For the first time I forgot my distance,
I took her in my arms and held her.

Waking up, I felt how alone I was.
I walked on the dock.
Fishing alone in the far north.

Black Pony Eating Grass

Near me a black and shaggy pony is eating grass,
That crunching is night being ripped away from day,
A crystal's sound when it regains its twelve sides.

Our life is a house between two hills.
Flowers stand open on the altar,
The moonlight hugs the sides of popples.

In a few years we will die,
Yet the grass continues to lift itself into the horse's teeth,
Sharp harsh lines run through our bodies.
A star is also a stubborn man—
The Great Bear is seven old men walking.

The Fallen Tree

After a long walk I come down to the shore.
A cottonwood tree lies stretched out in the grass.
This tree knocked down by lightning—
And a hollow the owls made open now to the rain.
Disasters are all right, if they teach
          men and women
To turn their hollow places up.

The tree lies stretched out
          where it fell in the grass.
It is so mysterious, waters below, waters above,
So little of it we can ever know!

Nailing a Dock Together

The dock is done, pulled out in the lake. How I love
Putting my wet foot
On the boards I sawed myself!
It is a ladder stretching back to land...

So many secrets are still hidden.
A walker digs up a tin box with secrets
And then joyfully buries it again
So that the night and day will remain fresh.

The horse stands penned, but is also free.
It is a horse whose neck human
Beings have longed to touch for centuries.
He stands in a stable of invisible wood.

Out Picking Up Corn

It is late December. I walk through the pasture,
Light on the hillocks, light
In the rolling mounds, eaten clean by horse teeth.

Then the black plowing, clods turned up,
The shoe looks for solid home.
A half covered ear of corn
Not found by a deer.

I am learning; I walk through the plowed fields,
With a bag, picking up corn for the horses.
Some small pebbles on the dirt road
Alight in the late sun.
Surely we do not eat only with our mouths,
Or drink only by lifting our hands!

Who is this out gathering moss by the sea shore?
"My master has gone picking ferns on the mountain."
No one knows what they were picking,
What they drink is something respectable people do not
Want to take in,
Walking in fog near the cliff.

For My Brother, a Year After His Death

Last night, full moon. I walked the roads
      where we played—
Walking between the plowed fields, silent and alone.
I thought of you, seeing black earth
Show clear above the new fallen snow,
Like riverbanks, above water, or the chest of
      graves.

from
Out of the Rolling Ocean
and
In the Month of May

Ferns

It was among ferns I learned about eternity.
Below your belly there is a curly place,
Ferns that hide deer, and I have learned to love
The curve that the deer's hoof leaves in sand.

Secrets

I walk below the over-bending birches,
Birches that arch together in the air.
It is an omen of an open door,
A fear no longer found in the wind.
Are there unions only the earth sees?
The birches live where no one else comes,
Deep in the unworried woods.
These sandgrains looked at by deer bellies.

The Black Hen

What we have loved is with us ever,
Ever, ever!
So you are with me far into the past,
The oats of Egypt...
Then I was a black hen!
You were the grain of wheat
I insisted on
Before I agreed to be born.

Returning Poem

Men bring the boat at night inside its slanted house by the shore;
Goats return when the farmer calls them to their earth-barn at
      night.
Brothers, working on different farms, go home after dark
And sleep together at last in the attic room under its slanting
      roof.
And the deer returns, finding her way through woods to her
      curving grass.

At night the man goes to the bus to meet the woman he loves—
It has only been a day—and impatiently brings her home.
So what was far out into the air, and the longitudes of the earth
Is brought home, taken in, a place prepared in the chest,
And the mountain loon returns, and soon is asleep in the
      mountain lake.

The Minnow Turning

Once I loved you only a few minutes a day.
Now it is smoke rising, the mushroom left by the birch,
The horse's forefoot, the way the minnow stirs silver
As he turns carrying his world with him.

Leaves on the Highway

Drops of rain fall into black fields.
Leaves fallen on the highway remain
Where they fall, and resist the wind.
A power neither of us knows has spoken to us.

I say a word or two, you answer a word.
We descended to some inner, or innermost, cave,
And this—as we woke today with faces wet
From overnight rain —frightens us a little.

Smoke of rain lifts from gravel roads.
Near barns rain water is gathering,
Other waters slowly join in woods.
Silent in the rain, no beginning or end.

Two People at Dawn

The sun orange and rose
Lights up covers and clouds.
Her head lies in his lap.
And his hand curves around
The bone box of her head.
Odor of candles
Floats in the room.

He says, "Our river flows
On a black mud bottom.
Are we walking there?
Are we under water?"
"We are under the ocean."
"Ah well," he says, "the ocean
Is only a slow river."

His hand remains firm.
Her courage shines
The whole length of her body.
The man joins her
In that briny place
Where cattle graze
On grass in the water.

from

The Moon on a Fencepost

The Moon

A solemn moon, nearly full, stands in the east,
Where we imagine Palestine to be.
A few birds flying. It is the sort of night
When children do not go home for supper.

The fence posts walk slowly around the field.
One post has a stone weighing it down.
Some mower, tired of having it in his sickle,
Lifted it there, balanced it, and left it.

Isn't it possible the moon is a stone?
But we don't know if it will stay.
Perhaps some day a man walking alone
Will find the moon by surprise in the grass.

Arriving in the North Woods

The last few miles were undisputed forest.
When I arrived, a light snow had fallen.
Up here where everyone is a failure,
The white ground answered the white moon.

I wanted to be alone in the useless woods.
Closing the car door I know that deer
Parked nearby hear it, and the wind
Moving through a thousand acres of bare trees.

I walk to the lake with my eyes on the ground
Over duff and poplar leaves. The curled edges
Of an oakleaf enclose a valley of private snow.
How long it would take a man to walk across it!

Moon Behind a Cottonwood Tree

Wind blows,
Hurrying
The cottonwood
Leaves,
Stirs them
Up, these
Tumultuous
Robust
Robber-brothers.
Soon the brothers,
Planning a robbery,
Are shouting.
A young
Woman sits
Among them
With pale
Face...
She never
Speaks...

Driving at Night

We drive for hours through the heavy spring darkness.
Finally a stop sign. Gas station lights
Turn the coarse ditchgrass pale.
An ordinary crossroads far out in the country.

Outhouses Near Appleton

The white schoolhouse lies anchored near the road;
Two white outhouses float to each side,
Like delicate outriggers.
Two thin paths worry away to each.

How marvellous to think of the two sexes
Each with their own separate bottoms
Out here on the treeless plains!
There are two sexes! It's fact!
It's a fact with a white door.
It's a fact with a hole beneath.

Error While Driving

All afternoon I drove through the snow-covered hills.
The power lines slant in,
      then shunt away,
As if into brooding.
A Finnish barn, still unpainted, over the fields,
Slips slowly along,
And the bushes along the fenceline move so fast!
Near Wadena I thought a black mailbox moving across the snow
      was a moose.

Spring

How long the evenings are in spring!
I walk about carrying an old stick.
The moon calms its part of the sky;
The clouds facing them do not move.
Cows are like boulders growing out of the field.

Windy Night in Summer

The weeping willow sends its shadows out;
They brush the grass again and again.
The wind once caught under the right
Horn of the moon is loose,
Making the barn doors rattle.

One man saw the moon come loose
From its place, descend
Toward him nearer and nearer.
He felt himself to be a small boy again
Fainting in his mother's arms.

from
The Apple Found in the Plowing
and
A Private Fall

A Private Fall

Motes of haydust rise and fall
With slow and grave steps,
Like servants who dance in the yard
Because some prince has been born.

What has been born? The winter.
Then the Egyptians were right.
Everything wants a chance to die,
To begin in the clear fall air.

Each leaf sinks and goes down
When we least expect it.
We glance toward the window for some
Thing has caught our eye.

It's possible autumn is a tomb
Out of which a child is born.
We feel a secret joy
And we tell no one!

The Call Away

A cold wind flows over the cornfields;
Fleets of blackbirds ride that ocean.
I want to be out of here, go out,
Outdoors, anywhere in wind.

My back against a shed wall, I settle
Down where no one can find me.
I stare out at the box-elder leaves
Moving frond-like in that mysterious water.

What is it that I want? Not money,
Not a large desk, not a house with ten rooms.
This is what I want to do: to sit here,
To take no part, to be called away by wind.

I want to go the new way, build a shack
With one door, sit against the door frame.
After twenty years, you will see on my face
The same expression you see in the grass.

Sadness

Dry winter grass stands upright still.
White flakes pause and fall into it.
Dogs circle before they settle. April:
The late spring snow swirling down.

Satisfaction

We have watched four winters from this window.
Snow falls on the horses slowly eating
And on the water tank overturned for winter.
The horses bend their necks toward the white ground to eat.

Living a Week Alone

After writing for a week alone in my old shack,
I guide the car through Ortonville around midnight.

The policeman talks intently in his swivel chair.
The light from above shines on his bald head.

Soon the car picks up speed again beside the quarries.
The moonspot on the steel tracks moves so fast!

Thirty or so Black Angus hold down their earth
Among silvery grasses blown back and forth in the wind.

My family is still away; no one is home.
How sweet it is to come back to an empty house—

The windows dark, no lamps lit, trees still,
The barn serious and mature in the moonlight.

Waking Up

When he wakes, a man is like the earth
Rolling over, as it rolls at dawn, turning
Jagged mountains gradually and grasslands
Up to the fierce light of space.

Someone in me remembered all night
To breathe on as I slept.
The breath protected me the way the atmosphere
Around the earth protects the earth.

When I was a small boy I like to think
I thought once it would be best to die.
That would make everything better
For others, and knives flew around the house.

At dawn I resemble a soldier who wakes after a battle,
His friends all dead, and himself still alive.
What do I do? I walk through the ditch grass,
Skirting the towns, asking in barns for fresh milk.

A Windy Pasture by Moonlight

I drive past the silvery grasses. The moon shines
From its hole in the sky, and wind
Bends the foxtails over and over.

Looking at the grasses, I go back
To some earlier life, another country,
A grassy country—miles and miles of grasses.

A hunter a hundred thousand years ago
Far out in the windy grass earth
Shouts to himself and leaps into the air!

from
Angels of Pompeii

The One Coming Closer

Who is this who is constantly coming closer?
It is the man in the ship's hold.
It is what the body knows, what it holds.

And this one who is constantly coming closer,
Ah, that is the spontaneous, mercurial one,
Imprisoned in the cedar root or the mustard seed.

He is no one we know: he is not Jehovah,
Or an obedient ermine-caparisoned king,
He is one nearer than near, closer than fingernails.

Are we all then religious? It must be so.
We know him, we see him, we hold him every day.
He is the one constantly coming closer.

The Blue Cube

It was midsummer. Something was waiting
Or being waited for.
I threw oatstraw bales in the afternoon
And then washed chaff from my hair.

In my dream last night I visited the ocean.
It was a far off place where the dead live
Hanging from trees, like the giant boas.
The dead hung exhausted but sleeping.

Toward dawn a cube of earth stood
Near me on a blue cloth, a cube
Of grief. Each time a man nudges it
With his shoulders, he goes one step higher.

Orion the Hunter

I found you floating in the night sky,
Sword-belted, gleaming above the farm:
A star man hunting wild stars,
Noticeable most when the moon is hidden.

When people like us look up to the stars,
They cannot tell what being is down
At their feet, what gives or is given,
What suffering shape may crouch there.

The Hunter drops his eyes to follow the tracks
Of his dogs, who follow the hare. But we,
Preferring—rightly—to know the stars do not
See the shape that dies to feed us.

from

Gratitude to Old Teachers

A Dream of William Carlos Williams

You were dead, but how sleek and darkly calm you were!
"There is some change," I said. Your wife said,
"There is a big change!" A third person was with us—
We all laughed about form, how sweet it is, *what*
It is! While you laughed, your rocker broke. "You fell

Out of it!" I shouted, but you were startled
To think of leaving form. As walked out
The back door and down the wooden stoop,
You asked about form in my poems. I found myself
Lying, saying I cared nothing about form...

Poem for James Wright

When I read your lines
I sometimes see, like
Hair on the back of hands,
Suffering
Grown out from between words.
Whole companies,
Battalions, died
In Guam. The surviving
Brothers drift on rafts
Scattered on the ocean,
Like the ocean-
People, going with the currents,
Sheltered
By one or two palm leaves
Shaped like ears.
You put your elegant
Language skiff into the brine,
As if to say, The octopus
Living in the grenade shell
Is still beautiful.

Wallace Stevens' Letters

Wallace Stevens comes hurrying down from the mountain
        calling for more tea.
He is stern this man whom I love,
Doubtful of the rocks on which he sits.
If the gods are all dead, then he should be mean...
And when he approaches, garden petals fall.
He walks, he thinks of God, he walks.
The terrible aging is over! The handsome dancer
Hurries in, stiff and stern and almost like a hero.

The Chinese Peaks

for Donald Hall

I love the mountain peak
But I know also its rolling
Foothills
Half-invisible
In mist and fog.

The Seafarer gets up
Long before dawn to read.
His soul
Is a whale feeding
On the Holy Word.

The soul who loves the peak
Also inhales the deep
Breath rising
From the mountain
Buried in mist.

The Gaiety of Form

I.

How sweet to weight the line with all these vowels!
Body, Thomas, the codfish's psalm. The gaiety
Of form lies in the labor of its playfulness.
The chosen vowel reappears like the evening star
There, in the solemn return the astronomers love.
When "ahm" returns three times, then it becomes
A note; then the whole stanza turns to music.
It comforts us, says: "I am here, be calm."

2.

"In the sad heat of noon the pheasant chicks
Spread their new wings in the moon dust."
When we choose so, the vowel has its own husband
And children, its nooks and garden and kitchens.
The smoking table gives plebeian sweets
Never equaled by the chocolates French diners
Eat at evening, and gives us pleasures, abundant
As Turkish pears picked in the garden in August.

Early Snow

It is snow, silence, the white birches whiter.
How sweet the soul feels with its heavy branches,
Weighted down by the snow, and no need to shake them off.
There will be more snow, more silence, more white air.

Bootmarks slowly grow classical in form, almost
Become Statius with his full-vowelled lines;
And it is all right for the twelve trees to remain.
This moment is already sweet, already gone.

An Open Rose

Why do we say that the rose is open? It opens as the road opens ahead of the traveler, as the water opens an instant after the diver has disappeared...the lion secretly feeds in the long grasses while still asleep in the cave. The grassy hollow is still hidden to which the red poppies on the slope lead us...Only the pheasant's head rises over the October grasses blown by new wind.

If I see water go over a rocky ledge, my urge is to follow after (we hear of those fatal accidents a few months after the friend dies). I feel the loneliness of "he who is not with us"—that place far inside the curling water, far inside the rose's petals. Where you go, I go...

Words with Wallace Stevens

You were so rash. I'd play saying
The gods have died, but I'd never say it.

Skeletons hold up Chinese lanterns
To ornament the party in Hartford

You wanted...You thought we could have
A coming-out party when the gods were dead.

You were a girl in love, a girl in a white
Dress, lolling in the garden, longing.... .

On the Oregon Coast

for William Stafford

The waves come—the large fourth wave
Looming up, thinking, crashing down—all
Roll in so prominently I become small
And write this in a cramped script, hard to read.

Well, all this fury, prominent or not
Is also hard to read, and the ducks don't help,
Settling down in furry water, shaking
Themselves, and then forgetting within a minute.

Remembering the fury, it is up to us, even
Though we feel small compared to the loose
Ocean, to keep sailing and not land,
And figure out what to say to our children.

The Exhausted Bug

for my father

Here is a tiny, hard-shelled thing. He is the length of a child's tooth, and clearly the fire of life is flickering out there. Its upper shell, the shape of a long seashell, wears its overlapping sidings, eight of them, all delicate brown, shaded as if it were some great cloth made for delicate wrists. The two antennae look bent and discouraged. When I turn it over with the tip of my Pilot ballpoint pen, the white legs move appealingly, even though my first response is confusion, as when we see the messy underside of any too-well-protected thing. It has twelve legs, six on each side, pale as tapioca. There are two pincers that come out to protect the head from hostile knights; or perhaps the pincers are meant to take hold of food. What else could they be?

I guess that it has exhausted itself, perhaps over weeks, trying to escape from this cloisonné dish on my desk. This dish is too little to hold a breakfast roll, and yet it is a walled Sahara to this creature, some courtyard in which the portcullis is always closed, and the knights, their ladies, their horse-drangers always, mysteriously, gone.

The sharp lamplight lit up the dish; it is odd that I did not see him before. I will take him outdoors in the still chill spring air and let him drink the melted snow of late afternoon on this day when I have written of my father stretched out in his coffin.

from
Holes the Crickets
Have Eaten in Blankets

On Assateague Island

November evening
Makes dusky
The dunes,
Gray sand
Deepens
And goes farther away.
I seldom speak
My grief,
I think it under
The water,
Turn it over
And over.
Herds of wild ponies
Leave hoofmarks
Up and down
This long
Forty mile island.
Some people respect
Only light
Streaming in
From distant stars.
I grieve
In Milky Ways
And speak
In single stars.
I keep this grief
To myself.
My words
Are a single
Horse,
With low belly,
Alone.

After Your Death

Sam, now where have you gone?
I held you often on my knees,
My arms circling you, and we
Were friends, helping each other.

In winter you worked late
Into the night, all one week,
Working Robert Frost's words
Into a cypress root for me.

Now the root speaks the words
You loved so well.
"Almost like a call to come in
To the dark and lament."

My Dream

I saw you nearly at dawn in a bath,
Naked in hot water, with your head thrown back.

"I was in the house of books, being washed.
It was in water almost too hot
For the three of us, being washed."

You added: "Dry me with your breath
For intense breath is prayer.
And it loosens the bonds of water."

December

Wind blows from the lake; the ponderous
Spruce boughs agree to talk about it.
But it's unlikely they will change their mind.

We turn our backs for a week in December,
We go to the city, never think of the snow at all,
And when we return the lake is frozen.

You dreamt last night that Sam put
The upper part of his body and his head
Down on the coffee table and wept.

The Bear and the Man

Suppose there were a bear and a man. The bear
Knows his kin—old pebbles, fifty-five-
Gallon barrels, pine trees in the moonlight,
Abandoned down jackets; and the man approaches warily—

He's read Tolstoy, knows a few symphonies.
That's about it. Each has lost a son. The bear's
Killed by a trap, the man's killed by a bear.
The boy was partly drunk, alone in the woods.

The bear puts out black claws firmly on earth.
He's not dumb. Skinned, he's like a man. People
Say that both bears and men receive a signal
Coming from far up there, near the North Pole.

Lake Sebago, Maine

The undersides of birch leaves seem so frail—
They turn their backs to wind and hurry away.

A man puts his foot on a bent birch near the cliff.
And the birch trunk sways under his foot.

The wind darkens the lake with cannibal thoughts.
The foam of each wave speaks, argues, and is gone.

The sandy water moves its bitter plans to land.
Death has won some argument with the little shells.

Holes in Our Speech

After having left blankets out on the grass all night,
I notice holes the crickets have eaten in the wool.
A man and a woman stretched out asleep
Will find the cold slipping in through those holes.

What we fail to see enters during the night.
It frightens the red-haired woman who brings
Her grey-haired lover to the Emergency door.
At the funeral people say: "How could we have missed it?"

Men and women build a house and live there,
And the roof falls if they let a single board go.
What we do not care to say fills the mouth
When we fail to speak a certain essential word.

Visiting a Cliff in Småland

> Persons in Viking times arranged on this Swedish cliff a
> group of stones in the shape of a long-ship.

Some few dandelions already turned into old men's heads
Stand around this ritual boat whose gunwales are stone.

This growling ground must have been sweet to the rowdy men
And women who woke, saved from glowering hags in their sleep.

Dreams were more frightening then—God appeared sometimes
At night as a dog with one leg, a Hag's son, or a man-eater.

Men clambered into the boat, they slept, they snored, then
The Hag pulled them down out of their seats into the sea.

"Oh yes," the sailors say, "we are glad that doesn't happen
To us. We are safe here eighty feet off the sea."

The Abandoned Hermit's Cabin

Even though leaves die in fall, it's clear that birds
Still want to live. The wren weaves her nest,
The wild waters refuse all sober tasks,
The boy and girl hold new roses when they marry.

We go on believing that we remain
Welcome here: and our tongues keep wanting
To speak the words *he* and *she* and *our*—
Those sounds to which our throats remain loyal.

But this world we cling to is only an unroofed
Hermit's cabin—the hermit long dead, the stove
Turned over, stovepipes down, door
Hinges pulled out, quilts and dishes scattered.

Attempting to Answer David Ignatow's Question

I wish I understood the beauty
in leaves falling. To whom
are we beautiful
as we go?

We are beautiful to the Mother as we go.
There are mysterious roads in jade that
Old men follow,
Routes that migratory birds walk on,
The circle dances
Iron filings do,
The things we cannot say.
Salmon find their way to old beds;
Sleeping bodies are not alone.

Frost and His Enemies

When Robert Frost set down a poetic whim,
The darkness with open mouth went looking for him.

Flowers love sun; but larvae, even at noon,
In their murky pond are excited by the moon!

When a foot in a marsh works to get free,
Water fills up the hole immediately.

When Frost sat down to get a poem right,
He was a sandy place open to night.

He wanted to see white, even if it were a birch,
Or a patch of snow or the steeple of a church.

from

The Urge to Travel Long Distances

Introduction

I lived as child on a farm in western Minnesota, which I left in 1944 when I enlisted in the Navy. After the Navy and college and a few years in New York, I returned in 1955 to a farm a half mile from my childhood home as a young married man. I wasn't farming, but my wife and I were simply living in a farmhouse on some land my father had saved for me. I was amazed at the permission the land gave to be untroubled, to spend long hours doing nothing, to pay attention to the wind and the land only a few years removed from prairie. By then I had found the Chinese poets, and my models were the poems of Tao Yuan Ming. I modeled my poems on his relaxed poem songs but the deep culture he came from was probably missing in my poems. I gathered a group of these countryside poems for the collection called *Silence in the Snowy Fields,* which I finished in 1961. A number of poems still half-finished remained in manuscript form, and I added a couple of poems a year over the next few years. During those years, the Vietnam War was intensifying, and a number of poems about that suffering were included in *The Light Around the Body,* published in 1968. So what we have here are a few of the poems written and left in manuscript during that quiet time before the Vietnam War claimed our attention. Even in these poems I occasionally see a hint of the larger suffering:

> Late at night the farm resembles a houseboat
> Moored on the river, about to slip away.

I still admire the beauty of the Chinese models, which often give more attention to the beings of nature than to the disasters of human life.

Minneapolis, November 2004

Singing Late at Night at Chuck and Phil's Farm

While the green corn smolders in hazy summer,
We stay up singing by tables under trees.
What should we be doing?
There must be something!
And the one I love is lost among thieves!
Half the night around the table at Chuck's farm,
We sing "Red Wing," and "If I Had the Wings of an Angel."

Spring Night

Tonight, after riding, and translating a few poems
        from the Danish,
I sawed off wild shoots from the box elder trees.
In the spring night we are not content to be home.
We have urges to travel long distances in the misty dusk.

Saturday Nights in Marietta

I.
Wonderful Saturday nights with girls
Wandering around! New
Farm machinery standing
Quietly in the cool grass.

2.
Men admire the old timbers
Of the bridge for steadfastness.
But some young women find
These timbers far too mild.

3.
The girl by the theater seems
Cool—like crisp leaves that have just been
Raked together. And all the other
Girls nearby going up in heavy smoke.

Summer

1.

The moon hangs in mist over the sleeping corn.
I sit in the ecstasy of the late night
And listen to the crickets cutting up the night
Into small bits of darkness that are food for man.

2.

I remember everything that has happened like a long tail.
I see valleys cooled by pines in the Black Hills,
Cold and powerful moons, grass swaying at night,
Smoke with the odor of straw piles and burnt stubble.

3.

You will find your own image in the grain of wood,
In the dark translucence of trees in summer,
In the rooster's shadow, in the simple chanting
Of a jointed insect, and the kindly shine of screens.

Gnats

This cloud of gnats resembles
Ghost substance—
It changes
Shape, lifts or sinks.

They are too excited—
They can't be feeding.
So few days to live
And they spend it this way!

The Hills Near Darky, Wisconsin

We are nearing these stumpy hills
Of Wisconsin, with oaks on top.
Brown leaves surround each oak trunk,
Like something seen in deep sleep.
I grow dizzy and do not know why:
Round hills, greenish on the slopes,
Becoming brown at the top,
Rising from the wintry cornfields.

A Cold Rain in May

1.
Outside the rain falls steadily.
It is the earth going to sleep.
The earth is tired and the grass tired;
Now they move toward a cold sleep.

2.
It's like the sleep of water
In a well on some abandoned farm,
Water that will wait and wait
In the clay, and never see the light.

Fishing Bullheads with Louis Simpson

1.

I am writing these words with a pencil stub
I found today pressed under dirt near the car tire.
After midnight, I sit down on the stoop.
No badgers are around, the tips of the grass do not move.

2.

The full moon passes under clouds in the south,
Like a flashlight passes under a boat.
The horse stands moodily by the lilacs.
No branches move; the low bushes are still.

3.

Bullheads we caught at Marsh Lake Dam
Thrashed around all day in a ten gallon pail.
At supper, you and I saw they were still alive;
We put them back into a creek nearby.

4.

What does this say? That persistence finally wins out?
That cruelty diminishes after dark? It is summer.
Late at night the farm resembles a houseboat
Moored on a river, about to slip away!

The Visit of Two Birds

1.

The hawk sailed over the trees with the light through
        his wings!
What a joy I received when I looked up and saw
The hawk floating past with the sun through his wings!

2.

The air is clear. It is early summer.
The sun is passing through our bodies also.
That which made it clotted is gone.

3.

At noon I drove north thirty miles.
I found a place by the lake to be,
And sat there alone all afternoon.

4.

After I'd been alone four hours,
A heron, with the cry of those
Who awkwardly suffer, and are ignored,
Settled near me on the shore.

Looking at Some Ruts a Mile From Home

I.

Rain fell all night, and now
Water stands in the ruts of the farm road.
Turning I see the mud gleaming in two paths,
Going back where I came from.

2.

Where did I come from?
Two farm people, one weighted down with shortcoming,
The other light, eager and feathery,
Married to each other.

3.

I stand a long time
Looking at the two ruts running between mud
Eastward. A car last night, passing, pushed white
Pebbles up the rutsides.

4.

I've made a mess of things.
Whom can I blame?
Not either of these two,
Riding in their heavy car.

What Olaf Bull Said

Believe in happiness, Seiglinde, try!

—Olaf Bull

Happiness is the wind rising
In a field of young plants.

It is a new-fallen apple
Found in the dark earth

Far from the orchard
In plowing time.

October Maples

How much energy in the weeping willow
Blown by October winds!
The pines hold in their thoughts
And the little maples long for old men.

Floating on the Night Lake

For James Wright

The moon rolls on through the eastern sky,
High over the lake and the snowy earth.
How much the moon sees from its place in the sky!
It is just east of us, near the house of great light.

Talk and Low Clouds

For James Wright, 1961

I.

Clouds and talk. All afternoon while it rained
We talked: of Lorca, the broken father, children lucky
To get out of the house alive. Dark clouds hover above,
Massive, still rich with cold water.

2.

You gone, I see wisps of mist hurrying eastward
Eighty feet or so off the ground, passing
High over my head, wisps misty and frail,
Stark against the solid cloudbank higher up.

3.

These bits of mist seem bodies that expected to get
By without being seen, who celebrate now
Some triumph over the human race, and will return
Tonight to a single pine box in a closed room.

4.

I feel some fear in these layered clouds
That are traveling in the same direction as your bus.
A chill wind starts up; the west says it saw nothing.
Even the tassels of the corn look crude and earthbound.

November

1.

I galloped through the clover at dusk,
Over cold plants touched by frost.
In the west, the sun was setting ocean-
Ward toward its bed of black mussels.

2.

The tired farmer sinks deeper in sleep
And sees the tangled metal, the belt-buckle
Of his regiment, now bloodied on the boy
Caught in the teeth of the thresher.

3.

Geese call all night from the dark.
Half awake in the night, the sleeper hears
Gravestones flying through the stars.
The grass stiffens when the rabbit is gone.

4.

The cold pickerel snouts slide downward
Through layer after chilly layer.
In the orchard, frost-bitten apples fall
To the black heaven underneath the frozen grass.

Farm Scenes

1.
Snow falls in the feeding lot
All afternoon. Everything is white
Except for the dark lumps of hay
The horse has pushed away with his nose.

2.
We talk for hours. Long after midnight
I carry water to the chickens.
The flashlight sways over the snow
Like a single thought alone in the night.

3.
One rooster and five molty hens
Shift uneasily in their stall. The barn
Is shadowy—one or two
Strands of hay hang from the horse's jaw.

A Gift

I love once more what I have always loved—
Leather, thick and stiff, the odor of clover,
A wooden tongue between two horses,
Frozen mud in the farm yards.

Fall Night

Fall night: Assyrian cities
Of blackbirds asleep in the trees.
Rabbits stretch up, eating the late leaves.
Water goes farther down into the earth.
Clouds cover half the Milky Way.

Feeding the Horses

The blizzard starts. By dusk China's eyelashes
Are white. As I open the barn door, she follows
Me in. Her snow-blanket cracks and flakes off.

Elizabeth, Coltus, then Katherine, all
Step quickly in as if someone were behind them,
Bend their necks down, and eat from the bales.

Wind blows snow sideways across the yard.
Snowbanks change position from one hour
To the next; night appears unexpectedly here and there.

The trees are asleep. Only the barn remains awake.
Snow has sifted onto the chicken feed.
The chickens shift nervously; their roost seems too long.

As I put my hand on the house door, I look back and see
The water tank upturned for winter in the feeding lot.
It's all right. Our bodies will surely last the night.

from

Turkish Pears in August
and Other Ramages

A Note on These Poems

A few years ago, I began to hear inside the stanza individual sounds such as *in* or *air* or *ar* call to each other. An *er* is a sort of being that cries out. What could we call a union of a consonant and a vowel? The word syllable is a ridiculous name for it; it's too Latinate and mute. These particles have more energy than the word "syllable" suggests.

Hearing these cries put me into a new country of poetry. I was not hiking among ideas or images or stories, but among tiny, forceful sounds. What would happen if I adopted *in* or *ar* as the center of a poem? Decisions on content would then depend on that. I let that happen. For length, I settled on eight lines, which is larger than a couplet but smaller than a sonnet.

Every poem, of course, has to have images and ideas and some sort of troubled speaker. But I began more and more to shift attention to the little mouths that cry out their own name.

I eventually accepted *ramage* as a title for this brief poem. The word occasionally appears as the name of a movement during some French compositions for flute; it is related to the French noun for "branch." We can hear the root of that in "ramify."

The tunings of these things is like tuning on horseback some sort of stringed instrument from the Urals. Each time you try to add one more of the chosen sound particles, new sounds abruptly enter the poem, and one has to deal with them.

Night in the Garden

Dust made somnolent by pine branches holds
Up the dark-headed, dangerous psalm-singer.
He cures the sick, raises Lazarus from the grave,
Insists that only John shall be exalted.
Demons scatter salt on the stony ground.
These pains and wrongs have been here a long time.
He clears the stains from Thomas's coat, makes
Arrangements for a donkey in Jerusalem.

Women and Men

We'd like to know what women want — some want
Heaven and earth joined. Some men want sawn
Boards, roads diverging, and jackdaws flying,
Heaven and earth parted. Women love to see
Strangers fed, children fed and laughing,
Daughters in seats of honor, canvases with Venus
And a naked man, doves returning at dusk,
Cloths folded, and giants sitting down at table.

Krishnamurti and His Students

The young men reading Krishnamurti say no
To womanly joy, orioles, wagtails, mud,
Rancid songs, the hair of drowning persons,
Bare ankles, the brandy-breath lost in cold,
All the glee bandits feel by the ocean.
That's all right, but it's not the whole story.
Krishnamurti himself loved orioles and wagtails,
As well as handsome women and flooded fields.

The Old Stone on the Mountain

Grief lies close to the roots of laughter.
Both love the cabin open to the traveler,
The ocean apple wrapped in its own leaves.
How can I be close to you if I'm not sad?
The animal pads where no one walks.
There is a gladness in the not-caring
Of the bear's cabin; and in the gravity
That makes the stone laugh down the mountain.

"No Beginning or End"

No beginning or end, the bees as they wind home.
Are there bees with no pinions and no wings?
"I love you every day." "The peony opens all summer."
Wind finds its simple way
Over the ocean, where the sound of the sand
Makes the boy imagine women in the distance.
Two seals dive as a woman glances up.
There is moonlight in the inner house.

"Whitman, how many hours I have loved your vowels"

Whitman, how many hours I have loved your vowels!
It's a stair of sound, and a barefooted dancer coming down.
My master, my lover, my teacher! You call to death,
But death does not hear its clammy name.
The master sings like a dark rabbi
Among ocean herbs on the shore: "Press close,
Bare-bosomed night." Be blessed, teacher,
By the Torah and the Bible inside the naked seed.

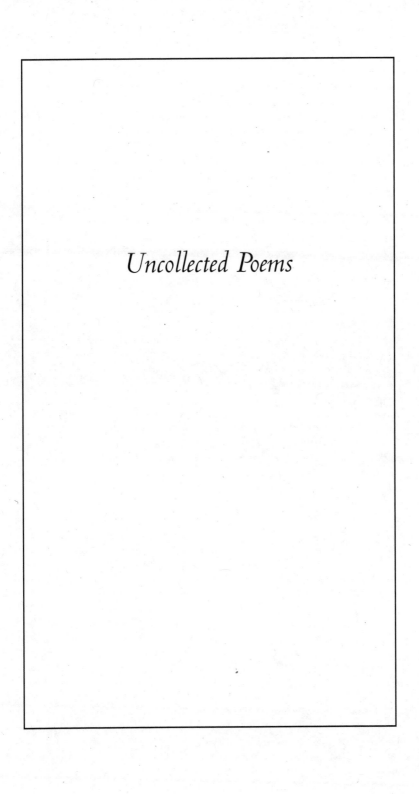

Uncollected Poems

Walking on the Shore in Late August

I look out over the muddy lake.
All at once I see a fin rise, what alertness!
All my brain power pours toward that spot on the water.
How we long for a bit of consciousness to appear above the
        water!

Now I notice what I have never noticed before,
Bending over, graceful,
At the shoreline...

Mother, take me deeper—
Take me on your fins down...

The Bear's Tail

1.

Herbs, turtle-faced porcupine babies,
Fur, paw marks on shore,
The hair in the mouse's ear.

2.

This delight is the wheeling of the inexhaustible
Bear, whose tail
Dips again and again into the ocean.

3.

We are like those rheumatic pilgrims, stalking
In the night air,
Driving flocks of angel cattle before them.

4.

And the molluscs, the mollusc shells, grow large.
Smoke twists up through water,
The moon rockets up from the sea floor.

5.

Long seeds drop into November loam.
The mother throws off her clothes, descending—
The Virgin is lost among the other stars.

On the Rocks at Maui

The Pacific water rushes in among the brown confident seaweed; over stones with whirl-holes the shape of galaxies! A black crab climbs up a searock sideways, like a demon listening in Aramaic.

I am not married, I have no parents, I wave my black claws and hurry over the rock, I love these with the seaweed clinging to them (they are stars), I am alone inside myself, I love whatever is like me, I leap out of the sea, I hold fast to a rock, no night-mother can pry me loose, I think my thoughts, I pray all day, and the seagrass, waving, is foolish, and I sway too, I withdraw into the desert and return, I never want, I hurry through the womb-systems at night, I meet shining boulders, I fail in sleep, in my dreams people whisper to me that I have lost their friendship, I sleep next to women, I wake.

Fall Solitude

I sit here, I have sat here all day.
I can feel my own breath enter and leave,
What is very old comes toward me flying slowly.
Alone for hours my hands become friendly to me.
Night gathers outdoors, the night inside slips over the sill, and
        goes to meet it.

Leaves slip down, falling through their own branches.
The tree becomes naked and joyful.
The leaves fall in the tomby wood.

Some men need so little (and I am one of them!),
Suddenly I love the dancers, leaping
Into the darkness, jumping
Into the air, and the singers and dancers and leapers!

Suddenly I start to sing, and rove around the floor,
Singing like "a young Lioun"

I want to rise far into the piney tops

And I am not going farther from you,
      I am coming nearer,
Green rain carries me nearer you,
I weave drunkenly about the page,
I love you,
I never knew that I loved you
Until I was swallowed by the invisible,
My black shoes evaporating, rising about my head...

A Moth with Black Eyes

A moth climbs down the sleeve of my sweater onto my left hand, as I write with the other. He waits there, among all the lamp-lit hairs. Then his antennae begin to move, as if a band were starting down the street, and he moves swiftly up my thumb—reaching the end, he turns around and goes back, and up the chest of my brown sweater.

Lamplight falls on his compressed, intense body, so self-contained, free of the longing for incest. How far he is out on the plain! His head is a haystack of brown fur, a hatrack with two mad gleaming eyes in front, and witchlike wands going out to either side, to poke into the other world, and see what the eyes cannot see.

And my big moving chest, what is it! I scratch the side of my nose, and a shadow falls across the chest. Outside the night goes on, on all sides into November, children are sitting near each other, on sofas, waiting for supper...

Alone in a Blizzard

It is the third day. The power has been out since yesterday. The horses stay in the barn. At four I leave the house, sinking to my waist in snow, push open the study door. Snow falls in. I sit down at the desk, there is a plant in blossom.

The upper petal is orange-red. The lower petal paler, as if the intensity has risen upward. Two smaller petals, like country boys' ears, poke out on either side.

The blossoms face the window where snow sweeps past at forty miles an hour...so there are two tendernesses looking at each other, two oceans living at a level of instinct stronger than mine...yet in them both there is the same receiving, the longing to be blown, to be shaken, to circle slowly upward, or sink down toward roots...one cold, one warm, but neither wants to go up geometrically floor after floor, even to hold up a wild haired roof, with copper dragons, through whose tough nose rain water will pour...

So the snow and the orangey blossoms are both the same flow, that starts out close to the soil, close to the floor, and needs no commandments, no civilization, no drawing rooms lifted on the labor of the clawhammer, but is at home when one or two are present, it is also inside the block of wood, and in the burnt bone that sketched the elk by smoky light...

A man and woman sit quietly near each other. In the snowstorm millions of years come close behind us, nothing is lost, nothing rejected, our bodies are equal to the snow in energy. The body is ready to sing all night, and be entered by whatever wishes to enter the human body singing...

Wild Hay

Moss on the snowy tundra,
The odor of wild hay,
The black eyes of the infant teal.

Mornings of Winter

Half-awake, we hardly know what we are!
We are the grass,
A light frost covers us.

Poem in One Line

The great ship falls against the dreamer's cheek.

The Land on the Tip of a Hair

The infinite lands that no one can describe
Gather on the tip of one of Buddha's hairs.
They don't nudge each other nor feel crowded
And the tip of the hair does not grow larger.
The lands all remain just as they were before.
The lands how do they enter the hair?
How huge the boundaries are!

Poem in One Sentence

So many things I love have been sent to Grenoble with the sea-
urchins.

Waiting for a Ferry in Northern Europe

Early dawn, the wind blows around the door of the car.
A fat Danish bird takes short leaps on the asphalt.
The sun makes boxes of light of the cars parked far off.
And the trucks, leaving the customs sheds with their covered
loads.

Looking Up at the Waterfall in Lofthus, Hardanger

How wonderful to look up and see water falling
Here it seems to come over the edge of the sky
And then drops to a lap, and then the long plunge
    after the slanting blow off the cliff

A deep plunge, loveless,
    floating,
it falls by the cliff
    like tufts of sleep

The sleep that overcomes the truck driver after having driven from
    the coast

The gestures in an animal's eyes when he dies in a room with human
    beings

Like the glimpses the meditator has of something floating under the
    water, neither moving or not moving,

Seeming to slow as it nears the bottom.

Picking Mushrooms in Late Summer in the Western Half of the Island of Runmarö with Tomas Tranströmer

The mushrooms loom in the grass like extremely stupid
    thoughts.
They are skies from which parachutes never fall.
From us, too, sometimes a poem falls, sometimes not.
Delighted to be together, we are out in the summer woods,
    picking mushrooms.

Doing Nothing Poem

My toes call over the dark peoples.
This poem will unwind from inside the reindeer's horn.
At that call the seas gather themselves
Together, as a man leaps out of bed!

Lying in a Boat, Troubled

I listen to the hull cut through the water,
Water hitting the hull
And being thrown back!
The sound
Is the snow falling,
The path down the mountain being slowly obscured.

On Top of a Colorado Mountain

Nearly sunset. I walked up two hours, reading as I paused. Now I am at the tree line. All around there are mountain tops with the light on them! The slight delicate Norwegian grass mountain-covering..... How I love its uncertain feminine green, all slopes and snow-pulled rolling valleys, all sublety and no speeches, all delicacy and no insistence, all music and no notes, all intimacy and no daydreams, all lovely absences and no angry presences, all faithfulnesses and no divisions...

The slate-gray mountain face plunges down, into the early heavy forms, (some snow there) as it dives down so sleekly, so calmly, into union... it must be that the descent into the furred ones goes along with the ascent into pure light...

I know there are hills inside me like these, and I want to walk on them, where the glad ones prance, holding on to the manes of horses, as the horses fly through heaven and hell, and turn into petals that fall onto the lap of the man with long ears reading... "The master is reading Sanskrit texts among falling flowers"...

Letting My Eyes Fall to the River

For James Wright

Eight steel cables painted silver climb
Their steep rise to the only, as you would say,
Medieval tower in Wheeling, West Virginia.
The cables, passing through
The tower, remind the bees to complicate
Their sight as they approach the bridge.

Below the tower a gray, solemn, muffled river
Passes by. Out of love for you, and
Your wildness, I have let my sight go
Down closer to the river, to glimpse
The faint disturbances — a fish or snag, perhaps,
Causing a whirlpool — drift by and out of sight.

In a Boat on Big Stone Lake

For Jack Maguire

I.

How beautiful it is, aging, to be out with friends
On the water! Already in June,
The water heavy with green filaments
Of life. Spring birds send in a warning
From the South Dakota shore.

II.

The briefness of life! How the yellow rope
Shines in the water-walking sun!
From inside us, deep ages
Walk across the water, buildings
Fall, the angel has spread its wings
Over the dark valley of tiny minutes.

III.

The country staggers toward light-
Hearted brutality.
We have made a long journey
And no one knows who is coming back.
I remember the muskrat's head, so sleek.
I remember something floating on the water.

ROBERT BLY was born on December 23, 1926, in Madison, Minnesota. He attended Harvard University and received his M.A. from the University of Iowa in 1956. As a poet, editor, and translator, Bly has had a profound impact on the shape of American poetry.

He is the author of more than thirty books of poetry, including *Stealing Sugar from the Castle: Selected Poems* (W. W. Norton, 2013); *Talking into the Ear of a Donkey: Poems* (2011); *Reaching Out to the World: New and Selected Prose Poems* (White Pine Press, 2009); *My Sentence Was a Thousand Years of Joy* (2006); *The Night Abraham Called to the Stars* (2001); *Snowbanks North of the House* (1999); *Loving a Woman in Two Worlds* (1987); *This Body Is Made of Camphor and Gopherwood* (1977); and *The Light Around the Body* (1967), which won the National Book Award.

As the editor of the magazine *The Sixties* (begun as *The Fifties*), Bly introduced many unknown European and South American poets to an American audience. He is also the editor of numerous collections including; *The Soul Is Here for Its Own Joy: Sacred Poems from Many Cultures* (1995); *Leaping Poetry* (1975); *The Rag and Bone Shop of the Heart: Poems for Men* (1992); and *News of the Universe* (1980). Among his many books of translations are *Lorca and Jimenez: Selected Poems* (Beacon Press, 1997); *Machado's Times Alone: Selected Poems of Antonio Machado* (1983); *The Kabir Book* (1977); *Friends, You Drank Some Darkness: Three Swedish Poets—Martinson, Ekelöef, and Tranströmer* (1975); and *Neruda and Vallejo: Selected Poems* (1971).

Bly is also the author of a number of nonfiction books, including *The Sibling Society* (Addison-Wesley, 1996); *Iron John: A Book about Men* (1990); and *Talking All Morning* (1980).

His honors include Guggenheim, Rockefeller, and National Endowment for the Arts fellowships as well as The Robert Frost Medal from the Poetry Society of America.

THOMAS R. SMITH is author of seven books of poems, *Keeping the Star* (New Rivers Press, 1988), *Horse of Earth* (Holy Cow! Press, 1994), *The Dark Indigo Current* (Holy Cow! Press, 2000), *Winter Hours* (Red Dragonfly Press, 2005), *Waking Before Dawn* (Red Dragonfly Press, 2007), *The Foot of the Rainbow* (Red Dragonfly Press, 2010) and *The Glory* (Red Dragonfly Press, 2015) He has edited several books, including *What Happened When He Went to the Store for Bread* (Nineties Press, 1993), a selection of the best of the Canadian poet Alden Nowlan, and *Airmail: The Letters of Robert Bly and Tomas Transtömer* (Graywolf Press, 2013). He is a a poetry instructor at the Loft Literary Center in Minneapolis. He posts essays and poems on the web at www.thomasrsmithpoet.com. He and his wife, the artist Krista Spieler, live in River Falls, Wisconsin.

DENNIS MALONEY is the editor and publisher of the widely respected White Pine Press in Buffalo, New York. He is also a poet and translator. His works of translation include: *The Stones of Chile* by Pablo Neruda, *The Landscape of Castile* by Antonio Machado, *Between the Floating Mist: Poems of Ryokan,* and the *The Poet and the Sea* by Juan Ramon Jimenez.

A number of volumes of his own poetry have been published including *The Map Is Not the Territory: Poems & Translations* and *Just Enough.* His book *Listening to Tao Yuan Ming* is forthcoming from Glass Lyre Press. He divides his time between Buffalo, New York and Big Sur, California.

Acknowledgements
Conltinued from copyright page

Most of the poems were previously published in the following books:
The Lion's Tail and Eyes (1962) - The Sixties Press

Jumping Out of Bed (1973/1987) - Barre Publishers / White Pine Press

Old Man Rubbing His Eyes (1975) - Unicorn Press

The Loon (1977) - Oxhead Press

This Tree Will Be Here for a Thousand Years (1979) - Harper & Row

Out of the Rolling Ocean (1984) - Ally Press

In the Month of May (1984) - Red Ozier Press

The Moon on a Fencepost (1988) - Unicorn Press

The Apple Found in the Plowing (1989) - Haw River Books

A Private Fall (1995) - Melia Press

Angels of Pompeii (1991) - Ballantine Books

Gratitude to Old Teachers (1993) - BOA Editions

Holes the Crickets Have Eaten in Blankets (1997) - BOA Editions

The Urge to Travel Long Distances (2005) - Eastern Washington University Press

Turkish Pears in August and other Ramages (2007) - Eastern Washington University Press

Most of the Uncollected Poems are from:

The Land on the Tip of a Hair: Poems In Wood,
Selected and Carved By Wang Hui-Ming (1972) - Barre Publishers

Airmail (2013) - Graywolf Press

Talking All Morning (1980) - University of Michigan Press

The remaining poems previously appeared in magazines and in other sources, including broadsides and postcards.